3.99

54/04

3.99

54/04

Religions Around the World

Investigate the beliefs and faiths of people everywhere

ENCYCLOPÆDIA
Britannica®

CHICAGO   LONDON   NEW DELHI   PARIS   SEOUL   SYDNEY   TAIPEI   TOKYO

Religions Around the World

INTRODUCTION

Who is the Dalai Lama?
What religion requires men to carry a comb? Where was Buddha born?
What happened when Moses approached the Red Sea?

In *Religions Around the World,* you'll discover answers to these questions and many more. Through pictures, articles, and fun facts, you'll learn about the people, traditions, and diverse ideas that make up the many religions of the world.

To help you on your journey, we've provided the following signposts in *Religions Around the World*:

■ **Subject Tabs**—The coloured box in the upper corner of each right-hand page will quickly tell you the article subject.

■ **Search Lights**—Try these mini-quizzes before and after you read the article and see how much - *and how quickly* - you can learn. You can even make this a game with a reading partner. (Answers are upside down at the bottom of one of the pages.)

■ **Did You Know?**—Check out these fun facts about the article subject. With these surprising 'factoids', you can entertain your friends, impress your teachers, and amaze your parents.

■ **Picture Captions**—Read the captions that go with the photos. They provide useful information about the article subject.

■ **Vocabulary**—New or difficult words are in **bold type**. You'll find them explained in the Glossary at the end of the book.

■ **Learn More!**—Follow these pointers to related articles in the book. These articles are listed in the Table of Contents and appear on the Subject Tabs.

Britannica LEARNING LIBRARY

Have a great trip!

The head of the golden Buddha at the
Thiksey Monastery in the Ladakh region
of India.

Religions Around the World

TABLE OF CONTENTS

Belief in a Higher Power

There are many people in the world who believe in a god or gods. Others do not use the word 'god' but still believe that there are other, greater forces at work in their lives. The way groups of people worship these forces or their gods forms what we call a 'religion'.

Many different religions are practised around the world. Major religions today include Christianity, Islam, Judaism, Hinduism,

Worshippers in Nepal celebrate Buddha Jayanti, honouring the Buddha's birth, death, and Enlightenment.
© Macduff Everton/Corbis

Daoism, Sikhism, and Buddhism. Most religions try to answer the same basic questions: How was the world created? What is the meaning of human life? Why do people die and what happens afterward? Why is there evil? How should people behave?

Many religions have buildings set aside for worship. In these temples, cathedrals, mosques, and churches, activities such as prayer, **sacrifice**, and other forms of worship take place.

At different times in history, followers of one religion have tried to make others believe in that religion. Sometimes this was done by peaceful means. Often, however, it was done by force - sometimes by 'holy wars'.

For instance, between 1095 and 1292, European Christians led a number of **crusades** against Muslims. In these crusades Christians tried to take control of the holy city of Jerusalem and other places they associated with the life of Jesus Christ. Muslims also carried out holy wars, or jihads. At various times Muslims spread into much of the Middle East and parts of Europe and Asia.

Most religions, however, encourage their followers to live peacefully with people of other religions. And, in fact, they share many **aspects** in common. These include **rituals** to perform, prayers to recite, places to visit or avoid, days that are holy, holy books to read and study, and leaders to follow.

LEARN MORE! READ THESE ARTICLES...
BUDDHISM · ISLAM · JUDAISM

DID YOU KNOW?

India is the birthplace of several world religions. Buddhism, Hinduism, Jainism, and Sikhism all began there.

Roman Catholics worship together in a service called 'mass'. Here the mass is being led by Pope John Paul II, world leader of the church, in Saint Peter's Basilica in Rome, Italy.
© Vittoriano Rastelli/Corbis

6

SEARCH LIGHT

True or false? All religions have a single god.

Answer: FALSE. Some religions have one god. But others have many gods, and some have no god at all.

One World, Many Beliefs

How did the universe start? How did life on Earth begin?

For thousands of years people have searched for the answers to such questions. Some people believe that science will solve the mysteries. But in the earliest times, science could not explain natural events such as earthquakes and storms, day and night, and life and death. People believed that these things were the work of beings greater and more powerful than humans: the gods.

Stained-glass image showing a Christian artist's idea of God the Father, with angels.
© Royalty-Free/Corbis

Today many people still seek an understanding of life through the worship of a god or gods. They often feel that their faith helps them live better lives.

Some religions, such as Judaism, Christianity, and Islam, teach that there is only one God, a **supreme** being who made the universe and controls the world. This is called 'monotheism', from the Greek words for 'one' and 'God'. The worship of several powerful gods is called 'polytheism', because 'poly' means 'many'. Ancient Greeks and Romans believed in many gods, whom we know today from ancient **myths** and art.

People from different places and cultures have their own names for their gods. The God of the ancient Jews was called Yahweh. Muslims use the Arabic word for God, Allah. Hindus believe in a large number of gods and goddesses (female gods). Each of them has a different personality and controls a different **aspect** of life. They believe these gods are forms of one supreme god. One popular Hindu god is the elephant-headed Ganesha. Many Hindus appeal to Ganesha when they begin an important new project.

The behaviour of a god can vary from religion to religion. Some religions may see their god or gods as unforgiving and cruel. Others consider their god to be merciful and kind. But all gods play a part in helping people understand their world.

DID YOU KNOW?

Not only did the ancient Egyptians believe in a large family of gods, but they also believed that their pharaoh, or king, was a god.

LEARN MORE! READ THESE ARTICLES...
HINDUISM · ISLAM · JUDAISM

SEARCH LIGHT

Fill in
the gap:
The Hindu god
of successful
beginnings
is _____.

In many world religions, worshippers like this woman in
Hong Kong burn incense to honour their gods.

© Royalty-Free/Corbis

9

A Life Apart

Most major religions have a tradition of monasticism. Monasticism comes from the Greek word for 'living alone'. So monks - men who practice monasticism - are people who choose to live apart from society. This allows them to devote themselves to a religious life. Women who choose this way of life are called 'nuns'.

Not all monks and nuns live entirely by themselves. Many live in communities with other monks or nuns. These community homes are usually called 'monasteries' or, for nuns, 'convents'. Life in a religious community generally focuses on prayer, **meditation**, and religious works. Monks and nuns may concentrate on building a personal relationship with God. They may work to purify their thought and reach spiritual perfection.

Some monks do live all by themselves as **hermits**. And some wander from place to place their entire lives. But whether they live

SEARCH LIGHT

True or false? Only Christians can be monks.

in a community or by themselves, all monks and nuns give up certain of life's pleasures. Many don't own property or have any money. Others force themselves to face certain challenges, such as **fasting** or other physical discomforts.

Monks and nuns choose to live apart so that they won't be distracted by life. Usually, they are unmarried, since having a family requires great dedication and time. The monastic life allows people to focus as much of themselves as possible on God and on the **salvation** their religion promises.

Many monks and nuns do still take part in the world around them. For example, they may serve as teachers, social workers, missionaries, or nurses. In earlier times monks were often among the few people who could read and write. So they're responsible for having preserved much of written world history and culture.

LEARN MORE! READ THESE ARTICLES...
DALAI LAMA · ROMAN CATHOLICISM · VIVEKANANDA

Answer: FALSE. Almost all the world's major religions have some tradition of monasticism.

Eternal Battle of Good and Evil

Over 2,700 years ago, a man named Zoroaster lived in Persia (modern Iran). At that time people worshipped many gods. Zoroaster's beliefs opposed this way of thinking.

Zoroaster denied the power of lesser gods and honoured one god as supreme - Ahura Mazda, also called Ormazd. The power of evil he named Ahriman. Zoroaster preached that a struggle between the two resulted in the creation of the world. Since its creation, the whole world has been involved in the battle between good and evil, light and darkness. Each human being struggles between good and evil. After a person dies, the soul crosses a bridge and passes into either heaven or hell.

Zoroastrians also believe that the history of the world is a vast drama divided into four periods of 3,000 years each. At the end of the first 3,000 years, the creation of the world takes place. At the end of the second, Ahriman arrives to corrupt the creation. In the third period, he triumphs but finds himself trapped in creation and doomed to cause his own destruction. In the fourth period, religion comes to Earth through the birth of Zoroaster.

Each 1,000 years thereafter, a new **prophet** will appear. The last of these will bring the final judgment and a new world.

Islamic armies invaded Iran about 1,400 years ago. Eventually, most Zoroastrians left Iran and settled in India around Bombay (now called Mumbai). These people came to be known as Parsis. The Parsis grew into a rich and highly educated community.

The holy book of the Zoroastrians is the *Avesta*. The central feature of their temples is a sacred fire that burns night and day and is never allowed to die out.

LEARN MORE! READ THESE ARTICLES...
GOD • ISLAM • RELIGION

SEARCH LIGHT

Who represents good in Zoroastrianism, Ahura Mazda or Ahriman?

DID YOU KNOW?
Zoroaster is sometimes credited with having created the practice of astrology. Astrologers 'read' the heavens in order to predict events and determine people's characters.

Between the ages of 7 and 11, children are initiated into the Zoroastrian religion in a ceremony called *navjote*. Here, priests oversee this young Parsi (Indian Zoroastrian) boy's *navjote*.
© Tim Page/Corbis

Answer: Ahura Mazda represents good in Zoroastrianism.

Religion of Israel

The Jews call themselves 'Israel', which in Hebrew means 'the people chosen by God'. According to Jewish holy writings, the one God promised Abraham, the father of all Jews: 'I will make of thee a great nation.' In return, that nation, Israel, was to obey God forever.

Later, when the people of Israel were enslaved in Egypt, a leader named Moses freed them and led the Jews to a new home. While going there, they made an agreement with God in the form of the **commandments**, God's laws. The commandments remind the Jewish people of their responsibilities to God and to each other.

Lighting the menorah in celebration of the Jewish festival of Hanukkah.
© Richard T. Nowitz/Corbis

All of this is written in the Hebrew Bible (known as the Old Testament to Christians). The most important section of the Hebrew Bible is the Torah - also called the Five Books of Moses, or Pentateuch. The Torah contains the religious ideas, history, ceremonies, and **rituals** of Judaism.

When a Jewish boy turns 13, he must read from the Torah in public. This makes him a Bar Mitzvah, or 'son of the commandment'. Girls celebrate their Bas Mitzvah, or Bat Mitzvah, which takes place after their 12th birthday.

Jews worship in synagogues, where services include the reading of the Scriptures, praying, and offering blessings and thanks to God. Important Jewish holidays are Purim, Rosh Hoshanah, and Hanukkah. The festival of Passover begins with a religious meal.

Today there are different groups within Judaism. **Orthodox** Jews dress, eat, live, and worship very much like their ancestors did hundreds of years ago. **Conservative** Jews worship much like Orthodox Jews but live by more relaxed rules. Reform Jews worship in more modern ways, with even fewer rules about how they live their daily lives.

LEARN MORE! READ THESE ARTICLES...
ABRAHAM • BIBLE • MOSES

SEARCH LIGHT

Correct the mistake in the following sentence: The most important part of the Jewish Bible is called the Bat Mitzvah.

Young Jewish boys all over the world celebrate their Bar Mitzvah. This young man carries the Torah at the Western Wall in Jerusalem as part of his celebration.
© Richard T. Nowitz/Corbis

DID YOU KNOW?

Many Jews 'keep kosher', which means they observe special laws about the food they eat. There are strict rules for how food is prepared and whether certain foods can be eaten in combination or at all.

Answer: The most important part of the Jewish Bible is called the Torah.

15

Father of Many Nations

The first book of the Bible tells the story of Abraham. This honoured leader is important in the major religious **traditions** of the Jews, Christians, and Muslims.

According to the account in the Bible, God came to Abraham one day and told him: 'I will make of thee a great nation.' God commanded him to leave his home in Mesopotamia (modern Iraq) for an unknown land, which would belong to Abraham and his descendants.

At the age of 75, Abraham started on this journey, bringing his wife, Sarah, and some other companions. They reached the **'Promised Land'**, then known as Canaan, in what is now Israel.

SEARCH LIGHT

How old was Abraham when he went on his journey to Canaan?
a) 175
b) 100
c) 75

Because Abraham and Sarah were so old when they settled there, they thought they couldn't have children. So Sarah gave Abraham her slave Hagar to have a child with, and Hagar gave birth to a son, Ishmael. But God had promised Abraham and Sarah their own child. When Abraham was 100 years old and Sarah was 90, their son, Isaac, was born. Sarah later sent Hagar and Ishmael away to live in the desert. Many consider Ishmael the first of the Arab people.

DID YOU KNOW?
Islamic tradition says that Abraham, assisted by his son Ishmael, built the Kaaba, the holiest of Muslim shrines, in the centre of the Great Mosque in Mecca, Saudi Arabia.

God tested Abraham by ordering him to kill Isaac as a sacrifice. Abraham was upset, but he was ready to obey. God stopped Abraham, however, and, because of his obedience, blessed him and his descendants. Isaac inherited the Promised Land after his father died and is considered to be the father of the Jewish people.

Abraham died when he was 175 years old and was buried next to Sarah. Abraham is still respected and honoured by Christians, Jews, and Muslims. They honour him as the father of their religion and as a great **prophet**.

LEARN MORE! READ THESE ARTICLES…
CHRISTIANITY · ISLAM · JUDAISM

Yahweh's Messenger

According to the Jewish Bible, the Hebrew people first went to Egypt in search of food during a great **famine**. Eventually, the Egyptians came to fear the Hebrews and enslaved them. At one point the pharaoh, the ruler of Egypt, ordered that all newborn male Hebrews be killed. Moses was born about this time, more than 3,000 years ago.

According to the Bible, Moses' parents set him afloat on the Nile River in a reed basket. The pharaoh's daughter found the child while she was bathing. Moses thus grew up in the Egyptian court. One day he learned that he was a Hebrew. He went out to visit his people and saw the hard life they led. Moses saw an Egyptian **overseer** beating a Hebrew slave, and he killed the overseer. He realized that he would have to flee.

Moses found shelter with a priest, married the priest's daughter, and became a shepherd. While looking after the flock, Moses heard God for the first time. God spoke to him from a burning bush on Mount Sinai, identifying himself as Yahweh. He told Moses to go back to Egypt and demand that the pharaoh set the Hebrews free.

Moses tried. But when the pharaoh refused, Yahweh punished the Egyptians with ten plagues. The tenth took the life of the pharaoh's eldest son, so the pharaoh ordered the Hebrews to leave.

Through much hardship, Moses led his people toward the Promised Land of Canaan. At Mount Sinai, Yahweh told Moses to go up the mountain. There Moses received the Ten **Commandments**. These laws and others told the Hebrews how to live. They became part of the Torah, the first five books of the Bible, and bound Jews to God.

LEARN MORE! READ THESE ARTICLES...
ABRAHAM • JUDAISM • MUHAMMAD

SEARCH LIGHT

True or false? Moses grew up in the Egyptian court of the pharaoh.

DID YOU KNOW?

The Bible says that as Moses and the Hebrews fled the Egyptian soldiers chasing them, they came to a body of water believed to be the Red Sea. Yahweh created a dry path for the Hebrews to cross, but he drowned the Egyptian soldiers who followed.

The famous artist Michelangelo created this sculpture of Moses, the founder of the religious community of Israel.
© John Heseltine/Corbis

Following Jesus Christ

Christians celebrate Christmas to honour Jesus Christ's
a) birth.
b) death.
c) resurrection.

More than two billion people around the world follow the teachings of Jesus Christ. They call themselves Christians. And their religion, Christianity, is the world's most widespread religion.

Christianity developed from Judaism about 2,000 years ago. Over the years it has split into many groups. This is because, at various times, Christians disagreed among themselves about some of their beliefs. The major branches of Christianity include the Roman Catholic church, Protestant churches, and the Eastern Orthodox church.

Despite the divisions, there are many things these groups agree on. They all have the same holy book, the Bible. The Christian Bible is divided into the Old Testament and the New Testament, which is about the life and teachings of Jesus Christ. Nearly all Christian churches have leaders, or clergy. In different churches they may be called priests, ministers, or pastors, among other titles. Clergy give their church members guidance and perform official duties at services of **worship**.

Most Christians believe in the Trinity as well. The word comes from Latin and means 'three'. It describes the three individual **aspects** of the one God. The three are: God the Father, who created everything; God the Son (Jesus Christ), who died to save humankind; and God the Holy Spirit, who inspires people's thoughts and actions.

And all Christians celebrate certain holy days. Christmas marks the birth of Jesus, and Easter honours Jesus' resurrection, when he rose from the dead. The Friday before Easter is called Good Friday. It is the anniversary of Jesus' death.

LEARN MORE! READ THESE ARTICLES...
JESUS CHRIST • MARY • ROMAN CATHOLICISM

DID YOU KNOW?
Although Christianity is widespread today, its followers were pursued and tormented in the religion's early days. Sometimes they were killed if they were discovered to be Christians.

Answer: a) birth.

The Son of God

Almost everything we know about Jesus Christ comes from the Christian Bible. Jesus was a Jew, born to Mary more than 2,000 years ago in Bethlehem. Christians believe that Jesus was the son of God. The New Testament **Gospels** of the Christian Bible tell the story of Jesus' life and teachings.

Jesus grew up in Nazareth, in what is now Israel. When he was 12 his parents took him to Jerusalem for the feast of Passover. Suddenly they discovered that he was missing. They finally found Jesus talking in the Temple with the learned men, who were amazed at how wise he was.

Like his earthly father, Joseph, he became a carpenter. When Jesus was about 30 years old, he began **preaching** about God. He is also said to have begun performing miracles. In one miracle Jesus fed 5,000 people with just five loaves of bread and two fish.

Jesus was kind to the poor and the sick. He was also kind to people who were disliked by others. He taught that all people should love each another just as they love their families and themselves. Jesus taught about the kingdom of God. Some people thought this meant that Jesus would try to rule a kingdom here on earth. The rulers of the land thought Jesus might try to seize power from them. So at age 33 Jesus was arrested, killed on a cross, and buried. But visitors to his tomb found it empty.

According to the Gospels, Jesus rose from the dead and was taken back up to heaven. First, however, he appeared many times to his followers. His followers became known as Christians, and their religion is called Christianity. They see Jesus' death as a **sacrifice** for all people.

Mosaic picture of Jesus Christ in the cathedral in Cefalù, Sicily, Italy.
© Mimmo Jodice/Corbis

SEARCH LIGHT

Fill in the gap:
Jesus taught that people should love each other as much as they love their families and _____.

LEARN MORE! READ THESE ARTICLES...
BIBLE · CHRISTIANITY · MARY

This stained-glass window in a church in Palo Alto, California, U.S., shows one of Jesus' miracles. This and other major events from Jesus' life are often subjects of Christian art.
© Steve Skjold/Photo Edit

DID YOU KNOW?
Throughout the history of Christianity, many people have claimed to have seen Mary. One of the most famous visions was reported in 1917 by three children at Fatima, Portugal.

Mother of Jesus

Christians worldwide honour Mary, the mother of Jesus. She is known as Saint Mary and the Virgin Mary. But not much is known about Mary's life. What we do know comes from the New Testament of the Christian Bible.

The Bible first mentions Mary as a young girl living in Nazareth, a town north of Jerusalem in Palestine (now in Israel). She was engaged to

A Pietà (image of the Virgin Mary and the dead Christ), by Luis de Morales.
© Archivo Iconografico, S.A./Corbis

marry Joseph, a local carpenter. One day an angel came to her and told her that she had been chosen to give birth to God's son. Later Mary gave birth to Jesus. King Herod heard that a newborn baby would one day become king of the Jews in Herod's own kingdom. Herod ordered all babies under the age of 2 to be killed. Joseph was warned by an angel in a dream, and he fled with Mary and Jesus to Egypt.

Mary appears again at the wedding at Cana, where Jesus performed his first miracle. She was also one of the few followers who did not run away in fear when Jesus Christ died on the cross. The New Testament Book of John describes how Jesus spoke to John and to Mary from the cross, telling them to look after each other. After that, Mary is mentioned as one of the people who devoted themselves to prayer after Jesus rose to heaven. She also took part in the early growth of the church.

But over the centuries, the mother of Jesus has become recognized as a holy person second only to Jesus in the Roman Catholic, Eastern Orthodox, and other churches. Her position has also influenced the lives of women in Christian cultures.

LEARN MORE! READ THESE ARTICLES…
CHRISTIANITY • JESUS CHRIST • ROMAN CATHOLICISM

SEARCH LIGHT

True or false? Saint Mary is Jesus' mother.

Mary, often called the Madonna ('Lady'), has been a favourite subject of artists for centuries. Images of Mary and the baby Jesus are a frequent theme, as in Fra Angelico's 'Madonna of Humility', seen here.
© Francis G. Mayer/Corbis

Answer: TRUE.

25

A Branch of Christianity

Christianity has been divided into many **denominations**, or different church organizations within one religion. Roman Catholicism is one of the oldest of these and has the largest following. It dates back to the 1st century AD, when it was founded by followers of Jesus Christ.

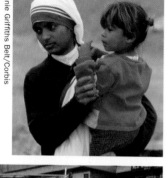

The headquarters of the church is Vatican City, located in Rome, Italy. The head of the church is the Pope, who is the **bishop** of Rome. He is the highest authority for all Catholics. The name Roman Catholicism comes from the religion's base in Rome and from a Greek term meaning 'universal'.

The chief worship service of the Roman Catholic church is called the 'mass'. The first part of the service involves readings from the Bible and a sermon, or religious lecture. The second half involves communion, when the priest stands at the altar and repeats what Christ did and said at his Last Supper on the night before he died. For Catholics the bread and wine taken during this part of the mass are the body and blood of Christ.

(Top) Nun of the order of Sisters of Mother Teresa, who help the poor worldwide. (Bottom) Catholic procession through the streets of Lagos, Nigeria.

Roman Catholics believe in holy people called 'saints' and seek their help in times of need. The most honoured of Catholic saints is Mary, the mother of Jesus. Like all Christians, Catholics consider the Bible the holiest of their religious books.

Catholics are expected to attend mass every Sunday and on major feast days, called 'holy days of **obligation**'. These holy days include Christmas, when Christians celebrate the birth of Jesus.

LEARN MORE! READ THESE ARTICLES…
BIBLE • CHRISTIANITY • JESUS CHRIST

DID YOU KNOW?
At one time, because of disagreements in the Roman Catholic church, there were two popes at the same time - one in Rome and the other in France.

26

SEARCH LIGHT

The word
Catholic
comes from
a Greek term
meaning what?
a) 'national'
b) 'universal'
c) 'local'

Roman Catholics everywhere celebrate mass.
These people worship in the historic Spanish
mission church of San José de Gracia in Las
Trampas, New Mexico, U.S. It was built in 1760.
© Craig Aurness/Corbis

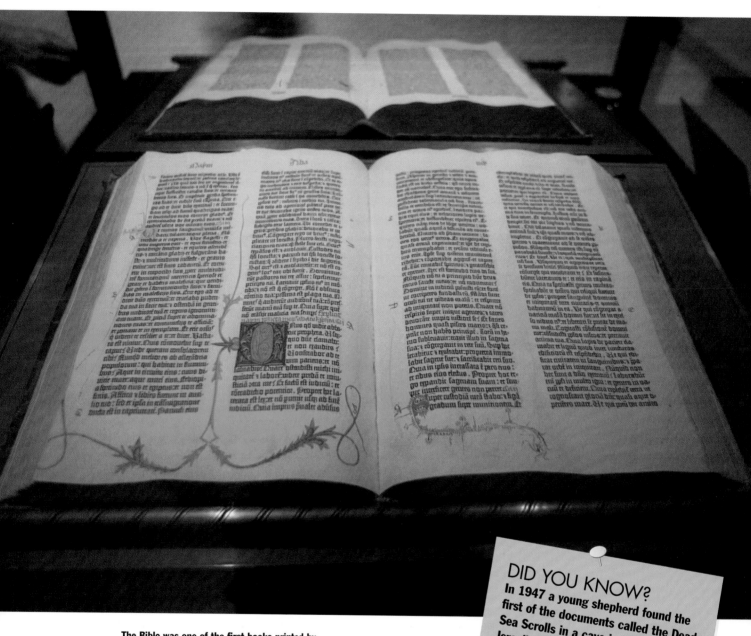

The Bible was one of the first books printed by Johannes Gutenberg on the first printing press. This is one of the few remaining copies.
© David Young-Wolff/Photo Edit

Jewish and Christian Scriptures

Jews and Christians call their scriptures, or holy books, the Bible. But their Bibles are not the same. What Jews call the Bible forms what Christians call the Old Testament. The Christian Bible also contains the New Testament. Both the Old Testament and the New are collections of shorter sections called 'books'.

© CLEO Photography/Photo Edit © Richard T. Nowitz/Corbis

The Jewish Bible tells the history of Israel. It is grouped into three sections: the Law, the Prophets, and the Writings.

The first five books, the Law, are

(Left) Family shares the Bible. (Right) Torah scrolls in the main synagogue in Jerusalem.

also known to Jews as the Torah. The Law describes how the world and people came to be and how Israel was founded. It contains the story of Moses, the Ten Commandments (instructions for life and worship), and other teachings. The section called the Prophets contains the later history of Israel as well as messages passed from God to the Jewish people. The Writings include history, songs and hymns, **psalms**, poetry, stories, and wise sayings.

The New Testament of Christianity tells the story of Jesus Christ and his followers. It is shorter than the Old Testament. There are four sections in the New Testament: the Gospels, the Acts, the Epistles, and Revelation.

The Gospels describe Christ's life, death, and resurrection (raising from the dead). In the Acts of the Apostles, the story and teachings of Jesus' disciples, or followers, are told. The Epistles are letters that various leaders of the early Christian church wrote. The Book of Revelation talks about the end of the world and the events that will take place before the end comes.

None of the original Bible documents still exist. The Bible **texts** are copies of copies that were handed down over many generations.

LEARN MORE! READ THESE ARTICLES…
ABRAHAM • CHRISTIANITY • KORAN

SEARCH LIGHT

Correct the mistake in the following sentence: The founding of Israel is described in the New Testament.

Answer: **The founding of Israel is described in the Old Testament.**

The Religion of Muhammad

SEARCH LIGHT

Which of the following is not one of the five Pillars of Islam?
a) fasting
b) prayer
c) faith
d) pilgrimage
e) singing
f) giving to the poor

Islam is a major world religion. It was founded in Arabia about 1,400 years ago by a man called Muhammad. Followers of Islam are called Muslims. There are more than a billion Muslims in the world.

Muslims believe that the archangel Gabriel brought Muhammad many messages from God (Allah in Arabic). Most people in Arabia at that time believed in many gods. But the messages told Muhammad that there was only one God. Muslims believe Muhammad was the last of God's prophets, in a line that began with Adam and continued through Abraham, Moses, and Jesus.

The messages to Muhammad were collected in a book called the Koran, or Qur'an. The Koran says that God is stern but forgiving and asks everyone to worship only him. Muslims believe that when they die, they are judged according to their actions.

Palestinian Muslim women pray during Ramadan outside the Dome of the Rock, in Jerusalem.
© AFP/Corbis

Islam has five duties that every Muslim should perform. These five Pillars of Islam instruct Muslims to make known their faith in God, pray daily, give to the poor, **fast,** and make a **pilgrimage** to the holy city of Mecca once during their lifetime if possible.

A Muslim must pray five times a day, either alone or with others in a mosque, the Muslim place of worship. Special group prayers are said in mosques every Friday. Fasting takes place during Ramadan, the holy month during which God is said to have revealed the Koran. During fasting, Muslims may not eat or drink between sunrise and sunset.

Mecca is the holy city of Islam where Muhammad was born and where Abraham built a shrine called the Kaaba. Only Muslims may enter Mecca. The yearly pilgrimage to Mecca is called the *hajj* and is celebrated in the festival of Id al-Adha.

LEARN MORE! READ THESE ARTICLES...
KORAN • MUHAMMAD • SIKHISM

Islam has spread throughout the world, as Muhammad had intended. These Muslims are praying together in a mosque in Sarajevo, in Bosnia and Herzegovina.
© Dean Conger/Corbis

DID YOU KNOW?

Medina, in Saudi Arabia, is celebrated as the first Muslim community. From there, Islam spread throughout Arabia. Only Muslims are allowed to enter the city.

SEARCH LIGHT

Fill in
the gap:
The messages
Muhammad received
from God were
recorded in the
_____.

Islam's Prophet

Muhammad was born in Mecca about 1,400 years ago. During his life he established Islam, one of the world's major religions.

Mecca was a **prosperous** and important centre of trade. Muhammad was a merchant and married a wealthy widow. When he was older, he spent many nights praying in a cave in a hill near Mecca. Muslims believe that on one such night he was visited by the archangel Gabriel, who brought him God's message.

Muhammad believed that God wanted him to deliver God's teachings to the Arab people. These teachings are recorded in Islam's holy book, the Koran. His family and friends accepted Muhammad as the last of a series of **prophets** of God that began with Adam and continued through Abraham, Moses, and Jesus. He then began to preach publicly in Mecca. His religion came to be called Islam, which means 'submission to God'. The believers were called Muslims, which means 'those who have submitted'.

Muhammad said that there was only one God, called Allah in the Arabic language. At that time most Arabs worshipped many different gods. Some people disliked Muhammad's idea and planned to kill him, so he moved to the city of Medina. In his new home he began **converting** people to Islam. After fighting a war with his enemies, Muhammad returned to Mecca and convinced everyone there to become Muslims. Many Arabs then became Muslims, and gradually Muhammad became the leader of Arabia.

Eventually, Islam split into different branches. All Muslims, however, look upon Muhammad as an example of an ideal of human life. They honour three cities connected with him: Mecca (his birthplace), Medina (the first Muslim community), and Jerusalem (which he supposedly visited on a journey to heaven).

LEARN MORE! READ THESE ARTICLES…
ABRAHAM • BAHA'I • ISLAM

The shrine known as the Kaaba, in the holy city of Mecca, is considered by Muslims to be the holiest place on Earth. The yearly *hajj* (or pilgrimage to Mecca) is undertaken by over a million worshippers. Daily prayers are said in the direction of Mecca and the Kaaba.
© AFP/Corbis

Answer: The messages Muhammad received from God were recorded in the Koran.

This beautifully illuminated (decorated) copy
of the Koran was made in the 18th century
for the sultan of Morocco.
© Corbis

SEARCH LIGHT

True or
false?
Muhammad
wrote down
the entire Koran.

Holy Book of Islam

Followers of the religion called Islam (Muslims) believe that God spoke to the Prophet Muhammad through the angel Gabriel. Muhammad received these messages for about 20 years. God, called Allah in Arabic, sent the messages so that Arabs would have a holy book in their own language. Muhammad and his followers memorized the messages and sometimes wrote them down. Altogether they're called the Koran, or Qur'an, which means '**recitation**' or 'reading' in Arabic.

(Top) Young Nigerian girl reads the Koran with other students. (Bottom) Students in Islamabad, Pakistan, at a *madrasah* (Muslim school of higher learning).

After Muhammad's death, Muslims were afraid that the knowledge in the Koran would be lost. So Uthman, the third caliph (Islamic ruler), ordered a single, official version of the Koran to be created.

The Koran's 114 chapters are not presented in the order they were revealed to Muhammad. The chapters are called *surah*s. The *surah*s have different lengths, but each begins with a prayer and is written in a poetic tone.

According to the Koran, there is only one God and all Muslims should obey God and his word. The Koran also reflects a belief in the **resurrection** from the dead, in angels and devils, and in heaven and hell. All people will be judged by God. The book also says that God's message to Muhammad is both a warning and a promise. It's a warning to those who refuse to believe in the one God. But it also promises spiritual rewards to those who believe in God and do his will.

For Muslims, the Koran is the true word of God and the final word in all matters of law and religion. It is also considered to be without any error in what it teaches.

LEARN MORE! READ THESE ARTICLES…
BIBLE · ISLAM · MUHAMMAD

DID YOU KNOW?

Many inside and outside portions of the Taj Mahal in India are inlaid with verses of the Koran. Calligraphy (artistic lettering) is a major Islamic art form. Some forms of Islam do not allow artistic images of living things, though the Koran does not mention this.

Answer: FALSE. Muhammad wrote down some of the holy messages he received. But one of Muhammad's successors, Uthman, ordered that the contents of the Koran be collected and written down.

A Simple Faith

The Baha'i faith is a fairly new religion with followers throughout the world. It grew out of Islam, the religion founded by Muhammad. After Muhammad's death, the Islamic religion split into two groups, Sunnites

Abd ol-Baha (Abdul Baha), first leader of the Baha'i faith, who is called the 'Center of the Covenant' and 'Architect of the Administrative Order'.
© Baha'i World Centre

and Shiites. Some Muslims (as followers of Islam are called) used the title of 'bab' (Arabic for 'gateway') for their religious leaders. The most famous use of the term was by a Persian (Iranian) Shiite named Mirza Ali Mohammad, who declared himself 'the Bab' in 1844.

One of the Bab's earliest followers was Mirza Hoseyn Ali Nuri, who took the name Baha Ullah. In 1863 he declared himself to be the messenger of God whom the Bab had predicted would come. Most of the Bab's followers believed him. Baha Ullah later founded the Baha'i faith. He made his eldest son, Abd ol-Baha (Abdul Baha), the leader of the Baha'i community.

The Baha'i faith teaches that a person's purpose in life is to worship God through prayer and meditation and seeks to unite all people in one religion. Those who follow this faith believe that people must also work to end racial, class, and religious unfairness. They believe that the founders of the world's great religions are all messengers of God. These messengers include Moses, the Buddha, Jesus, Muhammad, and Baha Ullah. They also believe there will be more messengers of God in the future. Followers of this religion do not drink alcohol, and they must seek permission from parents to marry.

Baha'i followers attend local spiritual assemblies to worship. There are also several impressive Baha'i temples located around the world. Baha'i services are extremely simple. There is no preaching. Instead, there are readings from the scriptures.

DID YOU KNOW?
Most Baha'i temples are nine-sided domes. These features suggest both the differences between and the unity of all people.

LEARN MORE! READ THESE ARTICLES...
BUDDHA · JESUS CHRIST · MUHAMMAD

The Baha'i House of Worship in Wilmette, Illinois, U.S., is one of seven throughout the world - at least one on each continent.
© Richard Hamilton Smith/Corbis

SEARCH LIGHT

Fill in
the gaps:

_____

was the
founder of the
Baha'i faith.

Answer: Baha Ullah was the founder of the Baha'i faith.

DID YOU KNOW?
Hindus consider the Ganges River, or Ganga, to be a holy place. Every year, hundreds of thousands of people bathe in the Ganges during a festival called a *mela*.

Ancient Religion of South Asia

Hinduism is a religion, but it is also a culture and a way of life. Over 800 million people, mostly in India and Nepal, practise Hinduism.

The roots of Hinduism go back more than 3,000 years. Since that time it has grown into many different **sects**. The beliefs of one Hindu might not be the same as those of another. But Hinduism is generally very accepting of differences between these subgroups.

Hindu devotees pray as they bathe in the holy Ganges River.
© AFP/Corbis

Brahman is the one supreme power in Hinduism, but most Hindus believe there are many gods. Most important among these gods are Vishnu, Shiva, Brahma, and Shakti. Each of the different gods has influence over a different part of life. For example, the elephant-headed god Ganesha helps remove difficulties. Lakshmi is the goddess of wealth. Shiva is one of the main and most complex Hindu gods. He both destroys things and rebuilds them.

Meditation is a very important part of Hinduism. It encourages relaxation and concentration to free the mind. Other forms of worship include chanting hymns and performing small **sacrifices** to the gods. There are also many holy books in Hinduism. The most famous and important one is the Bhagavadgita.

Most Hindus believe that human souls are reborn after death. The Hindu law of *karma* says that what a person does in one life affects his or her future life. In Hinduism the purpose of life is to do good things in order to free yourself from the cycle of rebirth.

Another important Hindu view is *ahimsa*, which means 'non-injury' to all living things. This has led to the well-known Hindu respect for the cow.

LEARN MORE! READ THESE ARTICLES...
BUDDHISM • JAINISM • VIVEKANANDA

SEARCH LIGHT

Fill in the gap. The Hindu concept of *karma* has to do with the cycle of _____.

The major Hindu goddess Kali is shown here in the Sri Veeramakaliamman Temple in Singapore. Like many Hindu gods and goddesses, Kali is described as having opposing qualities. For instance, Kali is linked with both violence and motherly love.
© Ted Streshinsky/Corbis

The Teacher of Hinduism

'**A**rise! Awake! And stop not 'til your goal is reached!' This was Vivekananda's call to the people of the world. His highest goal was to strive for self-perfection. And he felt that working to benefit **humanity** was the most honourable activity.

Vivekananda was born in India as Narendranath Datta in 1863. He was an active and curious child who questioned everything. He was fascinated by Hindu monks. He wondered how they could leave home and wander about the world.

'Have you seen God?' young Narendranath asked every holy man he met. He had heard people talk about God and pray to him, but no one said they had seen God.

One day, a holy Hindu man called Ramakrishna told Narendranath, 'Yes, I see God as I see you.' Sri Ramakrishna's honesty removed Narendranath's doubts.

Narendranath took the name Vivekananda, gave up everything, and travelled throughout India as a wandering monk. He felt very sad at the condition of the poor people of his country. He tried to find help to better their lives.

Vivekananda in 1900.
Courtesy of the Vedanta Society of Southern California

In 1893 Vivekananda attended the **Parliament** of Religions in Chicago, Illinois, in the United States. When he addressed the audience as 'sisters and brothers of America', everyone clapped. They listened as he talked about Hindu philosophy, about God, and about how all religions lead to the same goal of knowing God.

After travelling in the United States and in England for three years, Vivekananda returned to India with some of his Western followers. There he founded the Ramakrishna Mission. Still in service today, the mission works both to improve the lives of poor and uneducated Indians and to spread the vision of a Hinduism active in society.

LEARN MORE! READ THESE ARTICLES...
GOD · HINDUISM · MONASTICISM

SEARCH LIGHT

What was Vivekananda's original name?

Vivekananda founded the Ramakrishna Mission in 1897, the same year this photograph was taken. The next year, the Vedanta Society of the City of New York was founded. This organization is the oldest branch of the mission in the United States.
Courtesy of the Vedanta Society of Southern California

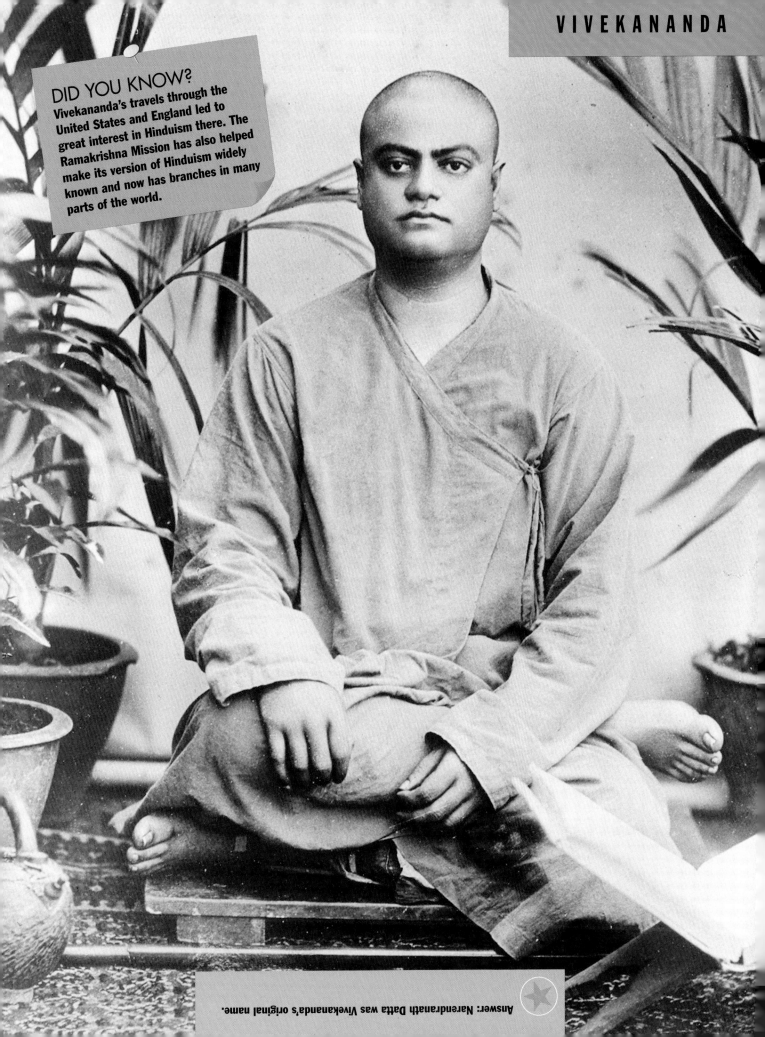

DID YOU KNOW?
Vivekananda's travels through the United States and England led to great interest in Hinduism there. The Ramakrishna Mission has also helped make its version of Hinduism widely known and now has branches in many parts of the world.

Answer: Narendranath Datta was Vivekananda's original name.

SEARCH LIGHT

Where did the Buddha live and teach?

DID YOU KNOW?

The Leshan Buddha in Sichuan, China, is the tallest statue of Buddha in the world, even though it is in a seated position. It is over 71 metres tall. More than 100 people can stand on one of the statue's feet.

In southwestern China, Buddhists may worship at temples such as this one in Kunming, in Yunnan province.

© Royalty-Free/Corbis

The Teachings of the Buddha

The religion that developed in ancient India around the teachings of Siddhartha Gautama, the Buddha, is called Buddhism. His teachings offered a way to achieve **Enlightenment**, and he attracted many followers. After his death, temples were built in his honour and his religion spread through much of Asia, especially China, Korea, and Japan. It has spread to Western countries too.

The Buddha taught about the Four Noble Truths, which became the basis of Buddhism. The First Noble Truth is that life is made up of pain and suffering. The Second Noble Truth is that all suffering is caused by a person's desires, by wanting. The Third Noble Truth is that a person can be free from these self-centred desires. The freedom from desire is called Nirvana, or Enlightenment. The Fourth Noble Truth is called the Eightfold Path.

(Top) Buddhist nuns in Dharmshala, India, where Tibet's Dalai Lama and others fled from their homeland in 1959. (Bottom) Student monks holding bowls to receive alms (offerings) in Bagan, Myanmar.

To follow the Eightfold Path means that a person follows a Middle Way between a life of luxury and a life of unnecessary poverty. Following this path eventually leads to a life free from suffering. The eight parts of the Path are: right understanding (of the Four Noble Truths), right thought, right speech, right action (including non-violence), right way of living (occupations in line with Buddhist beliefs), right effort, right mindfulness (attention), and right concentration (**meditation**).

The Buddha's teachings weren't written down until 300 years after his death. By then the religion had split into a number of groups, each with a different understanding of the Buddha's teachings. And today Buddhist monks, nuns, and priests carry the teachings forward as they understand them.

LEARN MORE! READ THESE ARTICLES…
BUDDHA • DALAI LAMA • SHINTO

The Enlightened One

The term 'buddha' means '**enlightened** one' - one who understands truths beyond the everyday world. It is not a name but rather a title of respect. 'The Buddha' or the name Gautama refers to the founder of the religion called Buddhism. If you see an image of him, he looks peaceful, wise, and full of love.

Gautama was the son of a king. He was born long ago near what's now the border of Nepal and India. His personal name was Siddhartha. Before his birth, his mother had a strange dream about a beautiful white elephant. The holy men predicted that the queen would have a son who would grow up to be either a king or a buddha.

When he was 29 years old, Siddhartha saw four sights that left him thinking about the purpose of life. He saw a weak old man with a walking stick. Another day he saw a sick man, and another day a dead body. Then Siddhartha saw a holy man looking very calm.

Siddhartha decided to give up the life of a prince. He left his home in search of truth. At one point he decided to sit under a tree until he became enlightened. He wanted to understand the truth about the spirit and about life. Finally, at the age of 35, Siddhartha reached enlightenment. He became the Buddha. The tree he sat under is called the bodhi ('enlightenment') tree.

Buddha spent the rest of his life teaching people a way of thought and living that involved **meditation** and a freedom from suffering. While he did not claim to be a god, some people do pray to him. Many people live their lives according to Buddhist teachings.

> **DID YOU KNOW?**
> The teachings of the world's great religious leaders often overlap. The Buddha taught that people should 'consider others as yourself'. Similarly, Jesus Christ taught that people should 'do unto others as you would have others do unto you'.

SEARCH LIGHT

Fill in the gaps. The word 'buddha' means '_____ _____'.

LEARN MORE! READ THESE ARTICLES…
DALAI LAMA · JESUS CHRIST · MUHAMMMAD

Answer: The word 'buddha' means 'enlightened one'.

SEARCH LIGHT

Which of the following is a good translation of the title Dalai Lama?
a) religious leader
b) yellow teacher
c) wisest teacher

DID YOU KNOW?
In 1989 the present Dalai Lama was awarded the Nobel Prize for Peace. This honoured his non-violent efforts to end Chinese domination of Tibet.

Tibet's Great Teacher

The word 'lama' means 'teacher' in the Tibetan language. Lamas are religious leaders who are usually great teachers or heads of **monasteries**. In the Mongolian language, 'dalai' means 'ocean', and stands for a vast 'sea of wisdom'. The Dalai Lama is head of the leading Tibetan Buddhist group called the Yellow Hat order. He's also the religious leader of Tibet.

Children observing the 14th Dalai Lama as he visits Sarnath, Uttar Pradesh, India, in January 2003.
© AP/Wide World

Until 1959, the Dalai Lama was the head of the Tibetan government as well.

Tibetans believe that some lamas are reborn as other lamas. The Dalai Lama is considered to be the human form of Avalokiteshvara. Avalokiteshvara is a *bodhisattva* (a Buddha-to-be) known especially for his kindness and mercy towards humans. The first Dalai Lama was Dge-'dun-grub-pa. All the Dalai Lamas that followed him are believed to be his reincarnations (rebirths).

How do the Tibetans know that the Dalai Lama has been reborn? The rebirth may happen days or even years after a Dalai Lama has died. Special attention is paid to a dying Dalai Lama's words and to any unusual signs during his death. Also, one special priest is believed to have visions and other **mystical** knowledge about a newly reborn Dalai Lama. A careful search based on these clues takes place. Often two or more boys may be examined before the new Dalai Lama is finally announced. The new Dalai Lama is trained at a monastery from an early age. A chosen adult rules the state until the young Dalai Lama has been educated.

Since 1959, the present (14th) Dalai Lama has lived in **exile** in Dharmsala, India. He and some followers left after a failed Tibetan rebellion against the Chinese government, which had invaded Tibet in 1950. Since then the Dalai Lama has worked hard but peacefully for Tibet's independence.

LEARN MORE! READ THESE ARTICLES…
BUDDHA • BUDDHISM • MONASTICISM

The present Dalai Lama teaches, lectures, and speaks to thousands of people worldwide. If he had not been exiled from Tibet, he would have led a quiet and protected life. But today he is a popular and well-spoken representative of the Buddhist religion and Tibetan independence.
© AP/Wide World

Answer: c) wisest teacher

DID YOU KNOW?
Jain non-violence includes insects. Many monks own nothing but a small broom to sweep insects from their paths and a mouth-and-nose covering to prevent them from swallowing or inhaling small insects.

Teaching Non-violence

SEARCH LIGHT

True or false? Jains are vegetarians.

Jainism is one of three major ancient religions of India, along with Buddhism and Hinduism. Jainism was founded more than 2,500 years ago by Mahavira. He probably lived at the same time as Siddhartha Gautama, who founded Buddhism.

The term Jainism comes from the word Jina, which means 'conqueror'. Jains believe that it is possible to fight earthly desires and physical needs to reach a stage of perfect understanding and purity. They work towards this **perfection** by taking vows that help them live properly. Jains try to reach a point where they no longer depend on the world or their bodies for anything. A person who reaches this stage is called a Jina.

In Jainism all living things have value. Jains believe in *ahimsa*, or non-violence, which means they cannot harm any living creature. As a result of this belief, most Jains are **vegetarians**.

Jainism has both **lay** followers (regular believers) and monks and nuns. All Jains are forbidden to lie, steal, and eat meals at night. But Jain monks

Jain worshipper pouring a milk offering on a huge Indian statue of Bahubali, the first human of this world-age to gain perfection and release from worldly needs.
© Chris Lisle/Corbis

and nuns also follow other very strict rules as they try to achieve a perfect inner state. They do not marry, and they keep few or no possessions. Most Jains are lay followers. They may marry, but they are expected to avoid certain foods and to keep few possessions. They are also expected to avoid unnecessary travel and pleasure, to **fast**, and to serve their fellow Jains, especially the monks and nuns and the poor.

Many lay followers also worship or make offerings to past Jinas and to various gods and goddesses. There are about 4 million followers of Jainism today in India and 100,000 in other countries.

LEARN MORE! READ THESE ARTICLES...
BUDDHISM • HINDUISM • MONASTICISM

This Jain priest stands before a statuette of Mahavira, founder of Jainism. His name means 'great hero', and he is honoured as the last of the 24 Jinas.
© Charles & Josette Lenars/Corbis

Answer: TRUE. Most Jains do not eat meat.

A South Asian Religion

SEARCH LIGHT

Which of the following is the holy book of the Sikhs?
a) Guru Nanek
b) *Adi Granth*
c) Amritsar

Sikhism is a religion founded by Guru Nanak in the late 15th century in India. The word 'guru' means 'teacher'. The word 'Sikh' means 'disciple' or 'learner'.

Guru Nanak was the first Sikh guru. There were nine gurus after him. The fifth Sikh guru, Arjun, wrote down his own **hymns** and those of the earlier gurus. The last guru, Gobind Singh (also called Gobind Rai), added his own hymns. He said that after his death the book in which the hymns were written would take the place of the Sikh guru. This book became the holy book of the Sikhs, called the *Adi Granth*, or *Granth Sahib*.

Sikhs call their places of worship *gurdwara*s ('gateways to the guru'). The chief *gurdwara* is the Golden Temple, built in 1604 in Amritsar, India.

Teacher helping two Sikh boys with lessons.
© Annie Griffiths Belt/Corbis

Sikhs eat together in the *gurdwara* as a sign of the equality of all kinds of people.

Sikhism includes **aspects** of two other religions, Hinduism and Islam. From Hinduism comes belief in a cycle of birth, death, and rebirth. Another Hindu feature is the concept of *karma*, which says that a person's previous life affects the present one. Islam's influence can be seen in Sikhism's description of God as the One, the Truth, the Creator, the immortal, the formless, and the ever present.

Most Sikh boys and girls will become part of the Khalsa, the Sikh **order** of soldier-scholar-saints. After that, men must not cut their hair, must wear short trousers (even under their longer outer trousers) and a steel bracelet, and must carry a comb and a sword. Sikhs are not permitted to use liquor, tobacco, or drugs.

LEARN MORE! READ THESE ARTICLES...
HINDUISM • ISLAM • MUHAMMAD

Much of Sikh worship is an individual activity. This woman - part of a Sikh settlement in New Mexico, U.S. - is meditating in her home.
© Buddy Mays/Corbis

Answer: b) *Adi Granth*

DID YOU KNOW?
Dance and drama play an important part in the activities of a shaman. The north Asian shaman becomes a fascinating sight, with his cloak floating in the light of a fire. He becomes actor, dancer, singer, and storyteller.

The Spirit World

A shaman is a person believed to have extraordinary powers. 'Shaman' means 'he who knows'. It is thought that a shaman can predict what's going to happen in the future. A shaman goes into a trance to enter the spirit world and performs special rituals to cure sick people. Because of this, the shaman acts as the people's doctor and priest.

Religious beliefs in which the shaman plays a major role are called 'shamanism'. However, the believers don't refer to their belief in this way. Shamanism is simply a term that groups together certain religious beliefs.

Shamans from Goshal village in northern India being greeted by Manali village elder (left) during festival.
© Lindsay Hebberd/Corbis

In general, followers of shamanism believe that everyone has a soul. A person falls ill when the soul leaves the body for some reason. It then becomes the job of the shaman to enter the world of spirits, get hold of the runaway soul, and bring it back to the body of the sick person.

It is believed that the spirits choose the man or woman who is to act as a shaman. The spirits first tell the person in a dream that he or she has been chosen. If the person refuses to become a shaman, he or she is made sick by the spirit until he or she gives in. People chosen as shamans typically have some unusual feature. For example, they might have an extra tooth or an extra finger.

People in very different parts of the world practise shamanism or have religions with very similar features. These include groups in North and South America, India, Australia, the Pacific Islands, and China. The greatest number of people who practise a pure shamanism live in northern Asia, mostly in the Russian region of Siberia.

LEARN MORE! READ THESE ARTICLES…
MONASTICISM • RELIGION • VODUN

SEARCH LIGHT

True or false? Shamans often have an unusual physical feature.

On the Southeast Asian island of Borneo, some people practise shamanistic traditional religions. Here a ceremonial dance is performed by a shaman of the Dayak people.
© Charles & Josette Lenars/Corbis

Religion of Magic and Spirits

Many people in Haiti believe in the religion known as Vodun or, among most outsiders, Voodoo. Vodun came to Haiti more than 300 years ago when large numbers of people from Africa were taken there to work as slaves. As time passed, the beliefs of the African slaves mingled with those of Haiti's French plantation owners, who were mostly Roman Catholics.

Those who practice Vodun believe that there is one god and many kinds of spirits, called *loa*. The purpose of Vodun is to serve these spirits and keep their goodwill. The spirits serve as a link between people and the god whom the Haitians call Bondye.

During ceremonies the *loa* may take control of (possess) a believer. That person then may do **ritual** dances, accept animal **sacrifices** for the spirit, and offer important advice to others. Otherwise the *loa* is a combination guardian angel and **patron saint**.

A Vodun priest is called a *houngan*, and a priestess (female priest) is called a *mambo*. They lead ceremonies in which people play drums, sing, dance, pray, prepare food, and sacrifice animals. The leaders also act as counsellors, healers, and expert protectors against sorcery or witchcraft. Important Vodun spirits are honoured on feast days of different Roman Catholic saints, and the spirits of ancestors are honoured on All Saint's Day and All Souls' Day.

Many Haitians believe in zombis. A zombi is either a dead person's bodiless soul that is used for magical purposes or a dead body raised magically from the grave to be a slave.

SEARCH LIGHT

Vodun is a mixture of African beliefs and what other religion?
a) Judaism
b) Hinduism
c) Roman Catholicism

LEARN MORE! READ THESE ARTICLES...
RELIGION • SHAMANISM • SHINTO

DID YOU KNOW?
Hollywood horror movies did much to create misunderstandings about 'Voodoo' and fear of its followers. It has often been shown as an evil and terrifying religion.

These women in Togo, in West Africa, are being received into the Vodun tradition in a secret ritual ceremony. Many people were taken as slaves from Togo to the West Indies, where Vodun is also a major religious tradition.
© Caroline Penn/Corbis

Teacher of Great Wisdom

Confucius was a Chinese teacher and thinker. He believed in understanding and learning, and in people's ability to improve themselves. In China, Confucius' ideas have been important for thousands of years. There, he is known as Kongzi, which means 'Master Kong'.

Confucianism is often called a religion, but it is really a system of **values** for living a good life. Confucius spoke more about goodness than about God. His teaching focused on how people could make themselves better in their lifetimes. He also taught about the importance of honouring one's parents and ruler.

Confucius was born to a poor family in 551 BC, more than 2,500 years ago. His father died when he was 3 years old. After that his mother educated him in music, shooting with a bow and arrow, arithmetic, chariot riding, and calligraphy (the art of handwriting). Confucius also studied Chinese poetry and history. All these things helped him become a good teacher.

In China during Confucius' time, parents sometimes hired special **tutors** to educate their

children. Only the wealthy could afford tutors, and poor children had fewer chances for education. Confucius wanted to make education available to all because he believed everyone needed to acquire knowledge and build character. He believed that education was the best way to understand yourself and improve the world.

Confucius spent his whole life learning and teaching so that he could change society for the better. Many of his wise sayings were collected in a work called the *Analects*. Today, many East Asian countries celebrate Confucius' birthday as a holiday.

LEARN MORE! READ THESE ARTICLES…
DALAI LAMA • DAOISM • JESUS CHRIST

DID YOU KNOW?
You may have heard of one of Confucius' famous sayings: 'A journey of a thousand miles begins with a single step.' What do you think he meant by that?

The Religion of Laozi

Over 2,500 years ago, there lived a wise **philosopher** in China. His name was Laozi. Laozi (also spelled Lao-tzu) lived in a time of battles and great social troubles. His teachings, therefore, offered a way to bring nature and human life into harmony.

The teachings of Laozi and others became the religion known as Daoism (or Taoism). According to Daoist tradition, Laozi wrote a book on Daoism known as *Daodejing*, or 'Classic of the Way of Power'. The main purpose of this book was to advise the king on how to rule his kingdom.

EB Inc.

The *Yin* and *Yang* symbol, suggesting the way opposites join to make up the wholeness of life.

Today Laozi is honoured as a saint by his followers in mainland China, Taiwan, Vietnam, Japan, and Korea. The followers of Daoism believe in the Dao (meaning the 'way'), which is understood as a natural force and the source of all things in the universe. In Daoism death is a natural process and results in a person's returning to his or her source, the Dao.

Daoism states that a human being is part of a universe based on the spiritual principles of *Yin* and *Yang*. *Yin* and *Yang* mean the 'dark side' and 'sunny side' of a hill. Together they create the wholeness of nature. A human being carries both *Yin* and *Yang* in his or her body and must balance them in daily activities through personal discipline.

While Daoism teaches the freedom of the individual, it also stresses the duties of the community toward its people and the duties of government toward its citizens. This is just one more example of the balance of Yin and Yang.

Daoism and Confucianism are very different systems. But together, for thousands of years, they have been major influences on Chinese culture.

SEARCH LIGHT

Daoism began in
a) China.
b) Vietnam.
c) Korea.

LEARN MORE! READ THESE ARTICLES…
BUDDHA • CONFUCIUS • SHINTO

During the Chinese New Year celebration, Daoists in Kowloon pray and make offerings at the Wong Tai Sin temple.
© Dave G. Houser/Corbis

DID YOU KNOW?
In Daoist belief, *Yin* is thought of as earth, female, and dark. It is represented by the tiger, the colour orange, and a broken line. *Yang* is thought of as heaven, male, and light. It is represented by the dragon, the colour azure, and an unbroken line.

In Shinto tradition, Inari is the god of rice cultivation
and merchants. The Fushimi Inari shrine near Kyoto,
Japan, is one of the most famous of many Inari shrines.
© David Samuel Robbins/Corbis

SEARCH LIGHT

True or
false?
In Shintoism,
forces of
nature may be
worshipped.

A Very Japanese Religion

Nearly all the followers of the Shinto religion are natives of a single country: Japan. There is no clear indication when Shinto began. It is basically as ancient as the Japanese people themselves.

Shinto is a loose set of beliefs and attitudes held by most Japanese about themselves, their families, and their ancestors. Shinto has no central holy book. No single group or individual created the religion. But its beliefs were strongly influenced by several Eastern religions. These include Confucianism, Daoism, and Buddhism. In fact, most Shinto followers are also active Buddhists.

Shinto monk visits shrine on Mount Haguro in Japan.
© Chris Rainier/Corbis

Shintoists honour and worship powers called *kami*. These may be gods, forces of mercy, certain ancestors, or other powers considered to be **divine**. *Kami* can't be known or explained. But they are believed to be the source of human life. And they guide people to live in harmony with the truth.

Each family or community has a specific *kami* that acts as the group's guardian. Many *kami* are connected to objects and creatures of nature, as well as to particular areas and family groups. Believers' own ancestors are also deeply honoured and worshipped.

Unlike many religions, Shinto has no regularly scheduled services or meetings for worship. Worshippers may visit their *kami's* **shrines** (or others) anytime they want to - some go every day. Several festivals and ceremonies during the year bring believers together. Shintoists celebrate births and weddings in special ceremonies.

The major Shinto celebrations are the Spring Festival, the Autumn Festival (a kind of harvest festival), and the Annual Festival (New Year celebration) with a Divine Procession, or parade. Each grand festival has a specific order of **rituals** to be carried out.

LEARN MORE! READ THESE ARTICLES…
BUDDHISM • CONFUCIUS • DAOISM

DID YOU KNOW?
In Shinto mythology, the sun goddess Amaterasu has long held a special place. She is the guardian *kami* of the Japanese royal house.

GLOSSARY

aspect part, feature, or quality of something

bishop churchman ranking above a priest who oversees other clergy and carries out other official functions

commandment law or rule for living

conservative tending to safeguard existing views, conditions, or traditions

crusade campaign or cause taken up with passion and belief

denomination religious organization based on beliefs; it joins church groups together to help govern them

divine holy, godlike, or concerning God

Enlightenment remarkably clear state of awareness, understanding, and inner peace

exile (noun) banishment or official separation

famine drastic food shortage, often ending in starvation for many

fast (noun) period of time when a person gives up or limits eating, often for religious reasons

Gospel one of the first four New Testament books, telling of the life, death, and resurrection (raising from the dead) of Jesus Christ

hermit person who has withdrawn from society to live alone

humanity the human race

hymn song of joy or praise, often to a god

layperson (adjective: lay) person who belongs to a religious group but is not part of its official clergy (as a priest or minister is)

meditation a quiet focused concentration, meant to calm and clear the mind; sometimes used to reach spiritual awareness

monastery a house for people who have taken religious vows, especially for monks

mystical having to do with a person's direct spiritual connection with a god or other supernatural power

myth story that unfolds part of the world view of a people or is used to explain a belief or natural event

obligation responsibility or duty

order religious community, usually requiring that its members take solemn vows promising duty and faithfulness

orthodox strictly obeying traditional rules, customs, or beliefs

overseer person in charge of others who are carrying out a task

parliament formal meeting for the discussion of a specific subject; also, a law-making body of government

patron saint holy person who is chosen to specially protect a group or place

perfection state of being without flaw or error

philosopher thinker or seeker after truth and understanding of basic concepts

pilgrimage journey made to a holy place to worship there

preach to deliver a sermon; to urge to accept an idea or course of action

Promised Land in Judaism, the land of Canaan, which God

promised to Abraham and Moses if the Hebrew people promised to worship only him

prophet a holy person who acts as a messenger between God and people; also, a gifted person with the ability to accurately predict future events

prosperous wealthy

psalm a sacred song or poem used in worship; especially, one of the biblical poems collected in the Book of Psalms

recitation act of speaking or reading a piece of literature aloud

resurrection raising from the dead

ritual the required form for a ceremony

sacrifice an act of offering something of value to save or make up for something else

salvation rescue from the power and effects of sin

sect group following a person or a specific set of beliefs

shrine place where honour or worship is offered to a saint or deity

supreme highest, best, and without limit

text written work

tradition custom; habit of belief or of living

tutor a privately hired teacher

values morals or ideals

vegetarian a person who does not eat meat

worship (verb) to honour and show surrender and obedience to a god or supernatural power